GINGERBREAD GEMS

VICTORIAN ARCHITECTURE OF OAK BLUFFS

ARTHUR P. RICHMOND

Schiffer Publishing Ltd

4880 Lower Valley Road Atglen, Pennsylvania 19310

Other Schiffer Books by Arthur P. Richmond
Lighthouses of Cape Cod & The Islands
Cottages of Oak Bluffs: 20 Postcards by Arthur P. Richmond

Other Schiffer Books on Related Subjects
Gingerbread Gems: Victorian Architecture of Cape May, by
    Tina Skinner & Bruce Waters
Gingerbread Gems of Ocean Grove, NJ, by Tina Skinner
Gingerbread Gems of Willimantic, Connecticut, by Michelle
    Palmer

Copyright © 2007 by Arthur P. Richmond
Library of Congress Control Number: 2007922602

Designed by John P. Cheek
Cover design by Bruce Waters
Type set in University Roman Bd BT/Aldine 721 Bt

ISBN: 978-0-7643-2682-0
Printed in China

Published by Schiffer Publishing Ltd.
4880 Lower Valley Road
Atglen, PA 19310
Phone: (610) 593-1777; Fax: (610) 593-2002
E-mail: Info@schifferbooks.com

For the largest selection of fine reference books on
this and related subjects, please visit our web site at
www.schifferbooks.com
We are always looking for people to write books on
new and related subjects. If you have an idea for a
book please contact us at the above address.

This book may be purchased from the publisher.
Include $3.95 for shipping.
Please try your bookstore first.
You may write for a free catalog.

In Europe, Schiffer books are distributed by
Bushwood Books
6 Marksbury Ave.
Kew Gardens
Surrey TW9 4JF England
Phone: 44 (0) 20 8392-8585;
Fax: 44 (0) 20 8392-9876
E-mail: info@bushwoodbooks.co.uk
Website: www.bushwoodbooks.co.uk
Free postage in the U.K., Europe; air mail at cost.

Acknowledgments

First of all, this book would not have been possible if it were not for the guidance and support of my editor, Tina Skinner. After publication of my first postcard book, *Lighthouses of Cape Cod and the Islands,* my suggestion of using postcards of the Campground was met with the response, "Let's do a book and call it *Gingerbread Gems of Oak Bluffs.*" This is part of the series that includes *Gingerbread Gems: Victorian Architecture of Cape May, New Jersey* and *Gingerbread Gems of Ocean Grove, New Jersey.*

To the friendliness and generosity of the residents, I owe a debt of gratitude. While I was walking the grounds and taking pictures, cottage owners would open their doors, beam with delight at possessions of another age, tell stories of a bygone time, and revel in a lifestyle few can imagine. To all the owners, thank you. To Virginia Hetherington, who wrote the Foreword, and her husband Arthur for their hospitality and willingness to give their time in sharing knowledge about the Campground. To William C. McConnell, Jr., General Manager of MVCMA, Sally Evans and Earl Jecoy who volunteer at the Cottage Museum, Randall Gerrard, Emerson Hovey, Jan and Paul Lofgren, George and Jean Jonis, Mr. and Mrs. Alfred Lilliendahl, Bill and Mary Moore, Mrs. Raymond Santinello, Tom and Nikki Surr, Frank and Theodora Olsen, Gloria Lee Wong and others who guided and aided me in this project, I cherish your support.

To Tony Pane, a special thanks for all your help.

To Noel Beyle, whose collection of old images is greatly appreciated.

To my wife, Carol, without whose help and support this would not have been possible.

Any errors of omission or commission are mine. Every attempt has been made to check for the accuracy of the information included. House numbers in some areas have been changed, more than once I found out, and I tried to find the correct one.

To Charley, my best friend.

Foreword

Spending summers in our Victorian cottage known as "Summer Love" in the historic Martha's Vineyard Campmeeting Association is special. Our cottage is one of 315 cottages that surround a Tabernacle in a park-like setting. This closely-knit community of people from all over the world enjoys spending summers together. Here, young people ride bikes and scooters, play games, attend Junior Camp, and enjoy making new friends. Parents, grandparents, and guests visit on porches, read, and enjoy a quieter life together.

The area has been a religious community since 1835 and the Tabernacle is the center for worship on Sundays. Distinguished preachers of all faiths are invited to participate in our services. In addition, there are spiritual activities and programs during the week. Camp sings take place regularly on Wednesday during July and August. Special programs are scheduled throughout the summer, attracting many islanders and visitors. Graduations, weddings, funerals, tours, art shows, a craft fair, and a flea market all add to events held in The Tabernacle. Upon entering the grounds of the Martha's Vineyard Campmeeting Association, one cannot help but be impressed by the beauty and quietness of the grounds beneath the ancient oak trees that attracted revival meetings in the early 19th century.

In the 1860s, when our cottage changed from being a tent into a wooden structure, daily living was quite different. Our house had fewer rooms and no plumbing or electricity. Today we have several rooms, two full bathrooms, an outdoor shower, and a modern kitchen with a dishwasher. We even have a washer and dryer. Porches were added in the late 1800s. Now we spend a great deal of time on our porch in our rocking chairs. Countless visitors from all over the world stroll by our pink and white gingerbread cottage decorated with over one hundred pink hearts. They take pictures and ask questions about the history of the Campground. Each of the cottages is unique in color and architecture. Of course, we tell them about the different rules that all of us must follow in order to maintain the integrity of our community.

Arriving in Oak Bluffs by ferry is like stepping into another world. Martha's Vineyard is an island filled with unique towns, beaches, restaurants, and a variety of shops. There are no Wal-Marts, McDonald's, Macy's or other regional and national businesses. Instead, one must settle into island life. Here people enjoy swimming, boating, fishing, visiting art galleries, attending shows and concerts, shopping, and just relaxing. Although we entertain family and guests throughout the summer, we feel like we are on vacation. Life at a slower pace is what everyone needs to experience. I hope you will make the time to visit the beautiful island of Martha's Vineyard.

—Virginia Hetherington

(Virginia Hetherington is on the Board of Directors of the Martha's Vineyard Campmeeting Association)

Contents

Introduction

Imagine a place of Victorian splendor not that far way, yet 130 years in the past. Such a place does exist: the Martha's Vineyard Campmeeting Association.

This special place had its beginning in a half-acre grove of oaks in what was then Edgartown. Reverend Jeremiah Pease was responsible for that first camp meeting in August 1835. Presbyterians started the first camp meetings but it was the Methodists that founded the campground on Martha's Vineyard. Living in primitive conditions, with food prepared and brought from home and no children present, the participants were involved in prayers and sermons morning, noon, and night. In that first year, "65 people were converted and five souls were reclaimed," according to one pamphlet. Popularity grew, and the Campmeeting known as Wesleyan Grove became one of the largest and best known in the country.

Most of the early participants came from southeastern Massachusetts. One reason why the community may have been so successful was its isolation. The only way to get there was by boat, hindering detractors of the camp meeting. By 1841, tents with families were starting to appear outside the main circle. In 1855, Methodist congregations or large societies occupied only 25% of the tents. Times were changing—participants would stay longer, children would become involved in religious activities, and living conditions would be improved. Wells were dug, buildings built, and businesses started to provide for the needs of the residents. Trinity Circle was built as a road in 1859. By 1860, there were over 500 tents and 12,000 participants attending services.

The first cottage was built in 1861 and by 1880, nearly 500 cottages had been built at a cost of $150 to $600. The most expensive was 10 Trinity Park at $3500. Many look almost the same today as they did back then, except for additions that have been added to the back of the cottages.

In 1866, the Association purchased more land, and today more than 300 cottages still remain on 34 acres that is The Martha's Vineyard Campmeeting Association. Also in 1866, The Oak Bluffs Land and Wharf Company was established, and with the purchase of land outside the Campground sought to develop a secular community. The lot sizes were larger, the cottages more ornate, and the residents more interested in a summer resort. Development would follow and Martha's Vineyard's premier resort would result.

In 1869, more than 30,000 people participated in Campground activities. The first Illumination Night was held that same year to honor the Governor of

Massachusetts. Originally sponsored by the Land and Wharf Company, it is now a yearly celebration in the Campground to mark the end of the summer season. In 1880, the two communities separated from Edgartown and became known as Cottage City. In 1907, that name was changed to Oak Bluffs and since then Oak Bluffs has been one of the most visited areas on the island. Throughout the years, numerous improvements have been made to improve living conditions, but the one circumstance that hasn't changed is the fabric of life within the Campground. Interestingly, cottage owners don't own the land; rather, they lease it on a yearly basis from the Association and taxes are also paid to Oak Bluffs. No work can be done on cottages during July and August. Originally Methodist, the Campground now is non-denominational. With only one in six cottages winterized, the Campground is in essence a summer community; Oak Bluffs, with larger cottages and many winterized, still remains a summer resort.

Visit the Campground and you will revisit the past, not as a visitor to Plymouth Plantation or Williamsburg, Virginia, or similar historical sites, but as an active participant in a thriving, energetic neighborhood. Participate in the numerous activities, enjoy the camaraderie and friendships, and—even more than that—acquire a feeling that life is good. The Martha's Vineyard Camp-Meeting Association was added to the National Register of Historic Places in December 1978, and in April 2005 was acknowledged as a National Historic Landmark.

This 1875 map is a plan for the Martha's Vineyard Campground Meeting Association and the lots where the cottages were to be built. The five-rayed structure in the center is the future site of the Tabernacle, which was built in 1879. The Trinity Methodist Church had not yet been built. What is obvious in this map are the curving streets, spokes radiating from a central focal point, and parks within rings of cottages on the outside. Around the various parks were the original tent sites, which later became cottages for the different congregations attending the revival meetings. This basic design was copied at other religious meeting areas throughout the United States.

The Campground boundaries shown here are the same today, as Siloam Avenue and Dukes County Avenue face Sunset lake, Lake Avenue faces Oak Bluffs harbor, and Circuit Avenue (not shown) is on the top left of the map. Close examination of the streets and neighborhoods will show that many have remained the same: Trinity Park, Allen Avenue, Central Avenue, Cottage Park, Forest Circle, and Clinton Avenue. Number one Trinity Park is the Cottage Museum. Other names have been changed: County Park is now Wesleyan Grove, Crystal Park is Vincent Park, Washington Park is Victorian Park, and Washington Avenue was renamed Butler Avenue. As you read this book, refer to this map in finding the location of the different cottages and parks.

The Martha's Vineyard Campmeeting Association

The Tabernacle

As one enters the grounds of Martha's Vineyard Campmeeting Association, the impressive Tabernacle looms as not only the physical but also the spiritual center of the Campground. It is the hub of activity, with religious activities, concerts, weddings, sing-alongs, lectures, and graduations all taking place there. During early camp meetings, a stage would be erected, used, and removed at the end of the week's activities. Through the years, more elaborate structures were built for the increasing number of participants.

In 1879, the year after the year round Trinity Methodist Church was built, the Board of Directors were also considering building a new wooden Tabernacle to replace the existing structure. Low on funds, the Directors proposed a structure that would not exceed $7200. Proposals for wooden structures were received and ranged in cost from $10,000 to $15,000. J.W. Hoyt, who had been a cottager for several years, proposed an iron building that would cost $6,200. Dwight and Hoyt of Springfield, Massachusetts, was awarded the contract on April 25, 1879 for a structure to seat up to 4,000 people and to be completed by July 1, 1879. The iron prefabrication was to be done in Springfield, then the framework, depending on size, would be shipped either by boat down the Connecticut River or by train to Woods Hole and then to the Campground.

With skilled workers, construction began June 1, 1879 and proceeded quickly, with the structure half completed by July 1. Once original benches were added, the first service was held on July 26 and the new Tabernacle was enthusiastically enjoyed. The final cost was $7,147.84. Hoyt, as designer and builder, added final touches including the stained glass windows. Today, the Tabernacle remains the largest iron building in the world. At over 140 feet in diameter and 100 feet high, it is an engineering marvel. As part of the Campground, it was added to the National Register of Historic Places in 1978 and in July 2000 declared an official project of Save America's Treasures.

The best way to experience the Tabernacle is early in the morning when only the sounds of nature are heard.

This early 1900s postcard view shows the Tabernacle with the Trinity United Church in the background.

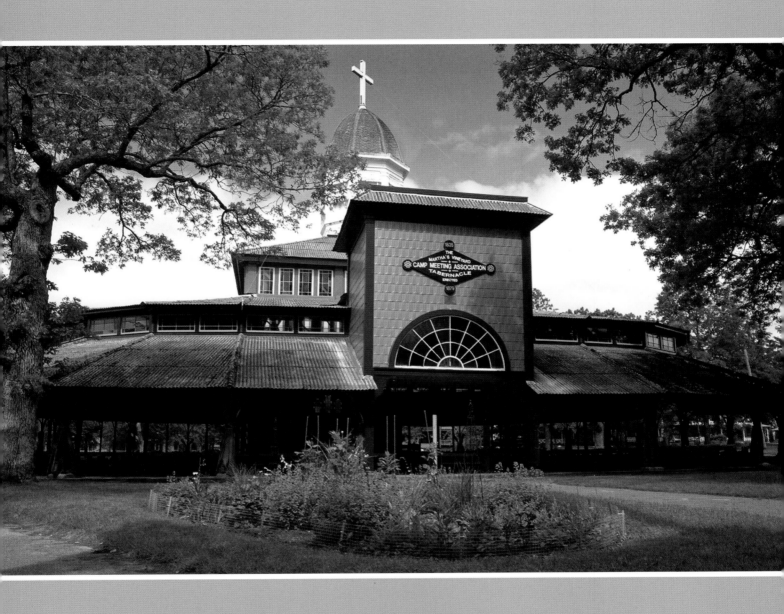

Compare this postcard view taken over 100 years ago with the present day images that follow.

These two modern day images display the iron framework built over 135 years ago. Note the Trinity Park cottages in the background.

From the balcony, the stage sits opposite the main entrance. The three roofs with stained glass windows between present an open airy forum. The four main supports are visible in this view. The grey benches are original and were present in the canvas tent before the Tabernacle was built.

This panel of stained glass on the front entrance to the Tabernacle was provided by J.W. Hoyt, the architect, during construction to add to the building's splendor.

First electrified in 1926, the cross is a beacon visible across Nantucket Sound. This gathering is celebrating Illumination Night, which marks the end of another summer season.

Trinity United Methodist Church

The Trinity United Methodist Church was built in 1878 and shares the green with the Tabernacle, built in 1879. As camp meetings became more popular and the season was extended, a year round church to minister to the visitors and residents became necessary. In 1871, a pastor was hired, and almost $8000.00 was raised to construct the church. It remains open year round for the entire community.

Compare the image of the church as it is now with a postcard image from the early 1900s; much of the trim and design are remarkably similar. Some of the peaks were struck by lightning and have since been removed. The original siding has also been replaced.

Interior walls and ceiling are made of the original stamped tin panels.

The stained glass windows lining both sides of the chapel are rectangular in shape and made up of numerous geometric designs.

Parish Hall

Built in 1885, Grace Methodist Chapel, located behind the Trinity United Methodist Church in Trinity Park, was planned as a building to be used by ladies' organizations within the Campground. It is still used in season for numerous activities, including summer school for the children. Much of the original trim is now missing.

Stained glass windows are found in the chapel, with flowers found above rectangular shaped panels.

The Cottage Museum

The first stop for any visitor to the Campground is the Cottage Museum, which is located at the corner of Jordan Crossing and Trinity Park. The address of the museum is one Trinity Park. Built in the early 1880s, the cottage allows for study of the internal construction as well as housing a wonderful collection of memorabilia, artifacts, and images dating back to the 1800s. Since the museum is open in the summer from Monday through Saturday and staffed by volunteers, it is possible to experience what life was like in Wesleyan Grove.

Originally, starting in 1835, tents were constructed in concentric circles radiating out from the Tabernacle, with different congregations having their own area for the weeklong religious revivals. With more and more people attending the meetings, the tents were replaced by wood-sided, wood-framed, and canvas roof structures. In 1840, twenty tents with wooden floors ringed a clearing where the religious meetings and services were held. The

first cottage may have been built as early as 1851, but was only temporary and little or no record remains of it.

The next step, by the 1860s, was construction of the Carpenter Gothic cottage, which emulated the original tents with double doors in place of tent flaps and distinctive windows like those found in churches. On a tent-sized lot, the cottages were constructed using mortise and tenon joinery, and since the wood used was long leaf yellow pine (which is high in resin), the cottages today are stronger and tighter than when built. Actual construction of the cottage was tent-like, with six four by four columns and two by six rafters. Smooth sided, random width boards were used for the sides and roof. Windows would then be cut out and the remnants used to make shutters for the winter.

The simplest cottages were one floor, with a sitting area in the front and an eating and sleeping room in the back. Kitchen and sanitary facilities, sometimes communal, would be found in the back. In two story cottages, the first floor would be partitioned off from the back room.

Several unique partitions are illustrated elsewhere in this book. Narrow stairs would lead to the second floor and any large pieces of furniture would have to be brought in through the front porch The second floor would be divided into a front bedroom with a porch (individuals could sit out there and watch the activities without being directly involved), a back bedroom, and an area between the rooms for storage. Kitchens would be moved inside as the cottages became more permanent.

By the mid 1860s, forty prefabricated cottages could be found throughout the Campground, along with an additional five hundred canvas tents. Many cottages were prefabricated off Martha's Vineyard and then transported to the island. It was also common practice to move cottages from one location to another within the Campground, to Oak Bluffs, or elsewhere on the island.

At present, there are slightly more than three hundred cottages, but only about fifty have been winterized and have full time residents. Even now, upon closer examination, several distinctive characteristics can be identified in the Carpenter Gothic cottage: the roof angle at the gable is 90 degrees; the bottom of the balcony porch marks the halfway point between the peak of the roof and the sill; the gable triangle is one third the height of the cottages; window and door dimensions remain the same in different cottages and reflect the original tent structure; the front of the cottages are highly decorated with vergeboard and brightly colored, while the other three sides have few windows and no decorations. Now, many residents have lovingly restored and maintained these cottages in the gingerbread spirit.

Located directly behind the porch, the living room was the main area where guests were entertained. Note the construction of beams and boards, which are held together with mortise and tenon joints. Also, note the image in the window of President Grant, who was a visitor to the Campground.

The front bedroom provided more than a sleeping area; with the distinctive doors and the balcony outside, it also provided access for the occupant to participate in the community.

In the original cottages, the kitchen and sanitary facilities were located outside, but over time the kitchens were moved inside and used by the individual families.

The back bedroom with the bed tucked under the eaves provided a sleeping area. Note the 2 x 6 rafters and smooth sided and random width boards. Since the cottages were only occupied in the summer, there was no need for insulation, and many still retain their original construction. Some, though, have added shingles to the outside as another layer of protection.

The shutters on this cottage have been made to fit within the window trim.

A third room upstairs, located between the two bedrooms, provided sleeping quarters for younger members of the family as well as space for storage.

21

Lawton Cottage

The first cottage believed to be built in Wesleyan Grove was the Lawton cottage at 70-71 Trinity Park. Prefabricated in Warren, Rhode Island in 1864, it was transported by sailing ship to Martha's Vineyard and erected at its present location.

Right:
The front porch was an extension of the living room, and the rockers allowed guests to be entertained. Many cottages, attempting to maintain privacy, currently use decorative chains and ropes to prevent access to the porch. Note the distinctive shapes of the windows and doors.

Center right:
The "Purple Lady," with its distinctive color scheme, sits in a row of cottages facing the Tabernacle.

Bottom right:
This side view of the Lawton Cottage shows the decorative peak with the trim on two levels. The shingles have been added to the original vertical boards, which can be seen on the front of the cottage.

Trinity Park

Trinity Park is the focal point of the Campground. Fifty-three cottages, with the Tabernacle in the center, form a ring reminiscent of the early Campground meetings. Most of the cottages have not been winterized and are only used during the summer season, and many retain their original characteristics, emphasizing the feeling of a bygone era.

As noted earlier, the first cottage may have been built as early as 1851, but no record remains of it.

Since the cottages had no foundations and were being bought and sold by members of different congregations, it was not unusual to have a cottage moved to a different location. Because of their small size, cottages would be moved within the Campground, outside to Oak Bluffs, and even further distances around the island. The cottages would be prefabricated off island, delivered, and constructed on site. Many builders would construct these cottages using the same basic design, from which the Carpenter Gothic style devel-

oped. Since Trinity Park is closest to the Tabernacle, most of the cottages were built and occupied by the most important Campground people, including preachers and church leaders; some cottages today are well known for their history. The history of others has been lost—given the decline of the religious meetings and numerous changes in ownership—although they remain summer retreats for the residents. Through the years, many of the cottages have been expanded by adding bedrooms, bathrooms, and the required necessities of modern living, including electricity and phone service. Some of the cottages are also available for summer rentals. Number one Trinity Park is the Cottage Museum, as discussed elsewhere.

Pride in ownership and a passion for the Victorian era has led to many cottages serving as outstanding examples of the gingerbread style of architecture. Porches, vergeboard, color schemes, and decorations vary within the neighborhood. To visit Trinity Park, is to step back in time and enjoy another age.

5 and 6 Trinity Park have different porches and different distinctive trims.

8 Trinity Park has a unique stair-like trim.

At $3500, 10 Trinity Park was the most expensive cottage to build. Known as the Ark because of its large size compared to other cottages and the rainwater that sometimes surrounds it, it was owned during the Civil War by Governor William Sprague of Rhode Island.

The porch of the Ark.

The Ark is also identified in the back of the cottage.

The porch at 12 Trinity Park.

14 Trinity Park with its distinctive tower.

Scalloped trim surrounds the second floor porch.

"La Dolce Vita," the cottage at 18 Trinity Park, was built in 1877 by J.W. Hoyt, who designed and built the Tabernacle. Stained glass windows on the second floor and an Italianate tower distinguish this cottage.

Porch at 18 Trinity Park.

Many cottages and sites are identified with plaques that indicate their historical significance. The Martha's Vineyard Campground Meeting Association and its cottages are on the National Register of Historic Places. In the background on Allen Avenue is the blue cottage called Tall Timbers.

20 Trinity Park is brightly colored in blue, yellow, and white.

Porch detail at 20 Trinity Park shows panels in the railing with center holes.

22 Trinity Park.

24 and 25 Trinity Park are neighbors but distinctively different in style.

Porch detail for "Purple Angel."

30 Trinity Park is hidden in the trees.

Built in 1867, "Bell Buoy" is nearly identical to its neighbor and is connected by a roofline and porches.

46 Trinity Park is larger than many of the nearby cottages.

57 to 62 Trinity Park are some of the closest cottages to the Tabernacle.

The same cottages are decorated in preparation for Illumination Night in mid August.

62 Trinity Park has three peaks, fleur-de-lis trim, and matching plants.

Porch detail, showing the etched glass door windows.

63 Trinity Park was named "Wee hoos" (Scottish for little house) by its owners, Mr. and Mrs. Thomas Surr.

The scalloped partition that divides the living room from the eating area is the only one of its kind in the Campground.

This interior view shows the stick construction, random width vertical boards, and doors similar to the tent openings. A Japanese lantern hangs to the right. Traditionally, when cottages are sold, the lanterns stay with new owners.

A stained glass window can be found on a side wall.

Lanterns and a sign are displayed during Illumination Night.

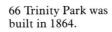
66 Trinity Park was built in 1864.

40

This row of cottages starting with number 67 extends towards the Tabernacle, which can be seen in the background.

72 Trinity Park was a tent site in 1858, then a cottage was built in 1866.

76 Trinity Park.

These two stained glass windows in 78 Trinity Park were originally found in the North Tisbury Baptist Church.

78 Trinity Park was destroyed by fire in 1973 and rebuilt by moving a cottage from another site.

The "Crumpet" at 79 Trinity Park is another unique cottage. To the right is the Association building.

The Martha's Vineyard Campground Meeting Association building, located at 80 Trinity Park, is a two-and-a-half story building that was constructed in 1859 for only $1000 and now houses the administration offices. Originally designed as a permanent structure to house the post office and meeting rooms, in the off-season it stored the gear and tents from the different church congregations.

The flag is on the Cottage Museum that stands at the end of this row of cottages.

The purple cottage at the far end of this row is the Lawton Cottage.

Several porches in Trinity Park.

This three story cottage on Allen Avenue is called Tall Timbers because the pine boards that provide support for the top two floors run the height of the house.

"Summer Love" Cottage

"Summer Love" at 15 Trinity Park is the summer home of Arthur and Virginia Hetherington, who are the sixteenth owners of this cottage built in 1867. Since 1992, they have added hearts to the cottage, which has four bedrooms and two kitchens.

The living room is not only partitioned off from the back but also from the side.

This original rocker has been in the cottage since it was built.

The front door trim has both obvious and more discrete vergeboard like heart designs. Many cottages identify the date of construction, but in this case, we also know L. Whitney Jr. was the builder.

A view from the porch of 15 Trinity Park. The Tabernacle is just to the left.

This is the only cottage in the Campground to have the original eight-sided balustrades.

The back porch.

Illumination Night is a celebration marking the end of summer, and many cottages are decorated with Japanese lanterns. Starting earlier in the evening, the Tabernacle hosts a musical event—with many sing-along songs—that is attended by thousands. As total darkness approaches and the Campground is in stillness, a signal is sent and the cottages one by one light their lanterns.

1 Hebron Avenue, built in 1873, features flowers in the trim and a large second floor porch.

2 Hebron Avenue is similar in design to the house across the street, but has two windows on the second floor porch. The cottage also has an address at 24 Rock Avenue.

This view of Hebron Avenue shows the only two cottages on the street. The pink porch in the background is a cottage found in Wesleyan Grove.

Tabernacle Avenue

The gate on Tabernacle Avenue leads into Trinity Park from Circuit Avenue, with the Tabernacle partially visible in the background. The letters on the side stand for the Martha's Vineyard Camp Meeting Association.

The cottage at 2 Tabernacle Avenue has a blue and white color scheme with squirrels in the trim.

Clinton Avenue was one of the last areas to be planned and developed; the cottages are larger and have more land than those found in Trinity Park. This row of cottages and pathway leads to the Tabernacle.

2 Clinton Avenue is the first house on a street just for walkers—no bikes, no cars.

This stained glass window is on the side of 2 Clinton Avenue.

Porch detail of 2 Clinton Avenue.

The yellow cottage at the left is 8 Clinton Avenue. Next door is the Bishop Haven cottage, at 10 Clinton Avenue.

8 Clinton Avenue now has a roof covered second floor porch, and may even be a different cottage than the one shown next to Bishop Haven in the 1880s view on page 59.

Built in 1869, this beautiful and restored cottage at 10 Clinton Avenue was owned by Bishop Gilbert Haven. A Methodist and anti-segregationist, he preached at the Campground.

Compare this stereoview image from the 1880s with the present view. Notice that a porch roof has been added and the balustrades on the first floor have been altered, but not those on the second floor. Also, notice the cottage in the background.

The side view of the cottage shows the continuity of the vergeboard trim around the house and a second floor side porch.

President Grant visited the island in August 1874 and stayed at Bishop Haven's cottage. He attended his Sunday sermon and saw fireworks from Dr. Tucker's cottage at Ocean Park.

These two views of the porch show details that are still present from the original construction.

23 Clinton Avenue.

25 Clinton Avenue has added dormers to the upstairs living areas.

This brightly colored cottage is number 29.

31 Clinton Avenue.

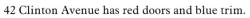

42 Clinton Avenue has red doors and blue trim.

46 Clinton Avenue

Porch detail of 46 Clinton Avenue.

50 Clinton Avenue is a large, expanded cottage.

Compare the porch detail in this view of 50 Clinton Avenue with the porch at 46.

In this view of 50 Clinton Avenue, the trim, porch, and door design are highlighted against the green house color.

56 Clinton Avenue.

With its peaks, trim, and distinctive color, 25 Butler Avenue ("The Pink House") is one of the most photographed cottages in the Campground. From the porch, it is possible to see Trinity Park.

Doves are found in the side railing.

The side of the house has the same pointed windows and doors with lace curtains.

THE PINK HOUSE

BUILT 1864

The Pink House was built in 1864.

Porch detail can be seen in this view.

69

The house at 24 Butler Avenue is one of the few cottages in the Campground that is almost in its original condition. The first floor porch without a railing surrounds three sides of the cottage.

Detail in the windows, door, and porch can be seen in this close-up view.

19 Butler Avenue is similar in design to 24, but has added a roof to the porch and a dormer to the upstairs.

15 and 13 Butler Avenue have different color schemes and porches but the same teardrop trim on the roofline.

4 Butler Avenue was built in 1869; the vertical boards can still be seen.

The trim on this cottage matches the bright flowers.

This neat small cottage is at 3 Butler Avenue.

The cottage at 1 Bayliss Avenue features five peaks, a decorative wraparound porch, and distinctive matching color scheme. Mr. and Mrs. Randall Gerrards have owned the cottage, built in 1869, for more than thirty years.

Porch detail of 1 Bayliss Avenue.

2 Bayliss Avenue.

This view of curving Central Avenue starts at Lake Avenue and leads into the Campground.

7 Central Avenue has two peaks, intriguing trim, and grapes in the upstairs windows.

This upstairs porch detail shows the trim, which includes a Martha's Vineyard shaped cutout.

The flying horse depicted here in the trim can be found around the corner at the Flying Horses Carousel (see pages 154-157).

12 Central Avenue, with lighthouses in the railing.

9 Central Avenue is a two story cottage with teardrop trim.

The pineapple in the peak symbolizes welcome and friendship at 5 Central Ave.

The porch at 4 Central Avenue.

Fourth Avenue leads into Trinity Park and has only a few cottages. This blue and white one is number 8.

A close-up of the second floor porch with swans in the eaves.

This side view of the cottage shows its flower covered arbor and the Wesley Hotel in the background with its original entrance.

9 Fourth Avenue.

This dog is found in the trim at 15 Fourth Avenue.

15 Fourth Avenue, with its extensive vergeboard.

Wesleyan Grove

Wesleyan Grove, named after the original Campground, is a neighborhood of eighteen cottages with a treed park in the center. Most of the cottages were built in the late 1860s, with residents often displaying these dates.

The pathway in this view is Chapel Lane, which leads to Trinity Park and the Tabernacle.

This view of several cottages shows the pathway that leads to Hebron Avenue and the harbor beyond.

Down this shaded pathway with hidden cottages is Montgomery Square and Circuit Avenue.

2 Wesleyan Grove has very distinctive roofline trim.

7 Wesleyan Grove is painted blue, yellow, and white; this color scheme is continued in the chairs and plantings.

This porch view shows the park and surrounding cottages.

The trim on the bottom of the second floor porch alternates boy and girl with a heart in between. The pointed door opens to a sitting area.

16 Wesleyan Grove.

Built in 1875, 14 Wesleyan Grove, with the original vertical boards, sits between its neighbors.

These four brightly colored cottages form part of the circle that is Wesleyan Grove.

19 and 18 stand side by side, but each is distinctively different.

The craftsmanship and detail can be seen in this second floor porch view of number 18.

The side of 18 has windows with decorative trim and lace curtains.

This stained glass window is found on the second floor.

4 and 2 Wesleyan Grove.

Vincent Park

Vincent Park is one of the smallest neighborhoods in the Campground, with only four cottages built in the late 1860s. Originally called Crystal Park, it was renamed in honor of Reverend Hebron Vincent, who preached during the summer religious gatherings. He was also significant in that he maintained a record of camp meetings from 1835 until 1869, when he passed away. Of all the areas within the Campground, Vincent Park most retains the feeling of a bygone era, as there is little evidence of modern conveniences.

This view of Vincent Park shows parts of the four cottages in the neighborhood.

12 Vincent Park is one of the larger cottages, with its two stories and porches.

Porch detail shows the original door design.

7 Vincent Park, built in 1870, is one of the few cottages in the Campground with a mansard roof.

Porch detail of 7 Vincent Park.

One of the smallest and least prestigious cottages in the Campground is 8 Vincent Park, which has been owned by Frank and Theodora Olsen for nearly forty years. Built in 1867, it is also one of the most interesting, with its tent-like doors, diamond shaped window that provides light for the loft, and teardrop trim. Its simplicity represents the original cottage design.

In this view of the cottage side, you can see the random width vertical boards used to build the structure.

This interior view of 8 Vincent Park shows the distinctive door shape, the stick frame construction with the posts and boards, a green Japanese lantern used during Illumination Night, and fishing rods over the door for use in nearby waters.

In winter, a lonely and cold day for the four cottages.

Cottage Park

The Cottage Park neighborhood is located directly behind Circuit Avenue. Like Clinton Avenue, it is only for walkers; no bikes or cars are permitted.

This early postcard image shows the area as it was over one hundred years ago, with a walking path between the cottages. *(Beyle Collection)*

2 Cottage Park, with its distinctive railing trim, has two second floor windows with no porch.

The porch railing at 3
Cottage Park has a unique
butterfly design.

3 Cottage Park.

8 Cottage Park is very similar in design to 2 Cottage Park.

12 Cottage Park is one of the larger cottages in the neighborhood.

15 Cottage Park, with its distinctive mansard roof.

16 Cottage Park.

17 Cottage Park.

Porch detail with
the pointing dog.

101

Forest Circle

This postcard image from the early 1900s shows Forest Circle and the cottages within this small park. *(Beyle Collection)*

Another view of the cottages within Forest Circle, showing the angled tree that may be the same as in the postcard image.

A wide angle view showing three of the cottages within the circle. Many changes have been made to the cottages over the years, making it difficult to match the postcard image.

Below:
Three cottages within the circle showing a variety in the trim, porches, and decorations.

Right:
This view shows 1 Forest Circle on the right and 15 Forest Circle on the left. There are only twelve cottages within Forest Circle and the empty spaces represent structures that once existed; this land can no longer be built on.

4 Forest Circle has a large second floor screened door that opens to the sleeping quarters. The roof trim is also very distinctive.

With its plantings and pathways, Forest Circle is a tranquil quiet neighborhood.

This cottage at 13 Commonwealth Avenue, built in 1869, is much larger and more expansive than the cottages closer to the Tabernacle. The decorative railing design is repeated on the first and second floors.

15 Commonwealth Avenue displays a side entrance to the porch; the rear of the cottage has been enlarged.

17 Commonwealth Avenue features a hunter and a dog in its trim. With the invention and development of power driven tools, it was possible to produce numerous designs and shapes that were used to decorate the porches and railings of the cottages.

This large, brightly colored cottage is at 26 Commonwealth Avenue.

11 Montgomery Square features a picket fence with an arch that leads to a cottage with decorative trim and a second floor porch.

Rock Avenue

As shown in this view, Rock Avenue is a circular street found behind Wesleyan Grove. Lanterns can be seen hanging on the porches in preparation for Illumination Night.

West Clinton Avenue

West Clinton Avenue was one of the last neighborhoods in the Campground to be planned and developed. Most of the cottages are larger with more land. This cottage is at 3 West Clinton Avenue.

7 West Clinton Avenue
has a second floor porch
with screens.

18 West Clinton Avenue.

One of the most brightly colored and decorated cottages is 22 West Clinton Avenue.

Porch detail of 22 West Clinton Avenue.

24 and 22 West Clinton Avenue.

Dukes County Avenue forms the western perimeter of the Campground; these three cottages exhibiting a variety of porches and trim are decorated for Illumination Night.

Three more cottages on Dukes County Avenue show different windows and doors.

This view across Sunset Lake shows the cottages on Dukes County Avenue with the Tabernacle on the right in the background. The steeple on the left is the Trinity Church.

An early postcard image of Sunset Lake showing the cottages with Trinity Church and the Tabernacle in the background.

From this porch, you can enjoy the view across Sunset Lake.

Lake Avenue

Lake Avenue forms the northern edge of the Campground, and these cottages face Oak Bluffs harbor. The building with the two green roofs almost at the end is the Attleboro House (see pages 127-129). The Flying Horses Carousel is at the end of this row of cottages and the Wesley Hotel (see pages 122-126) is directly behind to the right. Compare this view with the postcard view on page 125 showing Lake Avenue and the Wesley Hotel.

Nana's Dream is at 52 Lake Avenue.

58 and 56 Lake Avenue were both built in 1867 and are brightly decorated with Japanese lanterns in anticipation of Illumination Night.

46 Lake Avenue has two large porches and distinctive trim.

Also built in 1867 is this cottage at 60 Lake Avenue.

This single floor cottage in Victorian Park, built in 1876, has an extended roof that provides cover for the porch.

One of the objectives of the Campground's designers was to have cottages
set in park-like settings, as can be seen in this view of Victorian Park.

This large cottage at 3 Victorian Park has distinctive roof trim, a large porch, and an extensively landscaped front yard.

Facing the harbor at 70 Lake Avenue, The Wesley Hotel is the last remaining grand hotel built during the boom of the late 1800s. The original owner, Augusten Goupee, changed his name to Augustus G. Wesley and named the hotel for John Wesley, the founder of Methodism, the primary religion of the Campground. One of the first establishments built in 1879 for $18,000, and in continuous use ever since, the hotel has 95 rooms and is open from mid May to mid October. Originally, the hotel entrance faced Commonwealth Avenue and the Campground because that was where the activity was. In the early 1900s, the entrance was moved to the harbor side to take advantage of the views from the expansive verandas with their old-fashioned rockers. The Wesley was the first hotel on Martha's Vineyard to be wired for electricity. For many years, distinguished guests including Massachusetts governors would visit and partake in its Victorian elegance.

This 1910 postcard shows the Wesley Hotel with the distinctive W on the roof, which was blown down by a storm. Attempts to replace it have been met with opposition, and the room below now contains a cell tower.

This present day view shows nearly the same façade of the Wesley, but the sailboats have been replaced by modern day yachts. Reservations for many of the boat slips are made a year in advance and have been used by the same boaters for numerous years.

The Wesley Hotel before the docks were built can be seen in this postcard image.

Lake Avenue cottages with the Wesley Hotel in the background. Compare this view to the one showing Lake Avenue from the Wesley Hotel.

This postcard image from the early 1900s has the same row of cottages on Lake Avenue the Wesley Hotel in the background. Notice the trolley car on the tracks.

From the top floor of the Wesley Hotel, Fourth Avenue leads into Trinity Park, with the Trinity Methodist Church and Tabernacle in the background.

From the hotel's porch, Oak Bluffs harbor is across the street.

The lobby of the Wesley Hotel.

The fireplace and piano in the lobby of the Wesley Hotel.

Attleboro House

Besides the Wesley Hotel down the street, the Attleboro House at 42 Lake Avenue is the only other property in the Campground that provides accommodations. Two wraparound verandas allow visitors to sit and enjoy Oak Bluffs harbor.

First floor porch.

Second floor porch.

Looking towards the carousel are four neighboring porches.

Looking towards the Wesley Hotel at the end of this row of cottages.

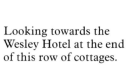

The Highlands

In addition to the Wesleyan Grove community and the Land and Wharf Company, a third area—in the hills to the north—was planned in 1868 by the Vineyard Grove Company. This area, known as the Highlands and designed by R.M. Copeland, features curved streets, triangular parks, and a central space for religious meetings. After 1875, Baptists would hold their summer gatherings here and in 1877 they constructed an octagonal tabernacle over 130 feet in diameter and 20 feet high to hold their services. It no longer exists, but remnants are visible on the ground. The current Tabernacle was built two years later and this earlier one may have inspired Hoyt in his design.

The Highlands today is a mixture of both Victorian cottages restored and maintained in their original condition and modern homes scattered throughout the area. It also has several stops on the African American Heritage Trail of Martha's Vineyard, where prominent doctors, writers, and politicians would summer.

6 Dorothy West Way retains an original window in the porch that has been closed in. This way is named in honor of Dorothy West, an African American writer and member of the Harlem Renaissance group.

In the same family since it was built in 1875, 12 John Wesley Way is now owned by Mr. and Mrs. Alfred Lilliendahl, who occupy it only in the summer.

10 John Wesley Way. This street was named for John Wesley, the founder of Methodism. It was the Methodists who held the first camp meetings in Wesleyan Grove. This area would eventually have a large Baptist population.

Also dating to 1875, this large expansive cottage was originally built and occupied by Captain William Philips, who transported coal along the coast.

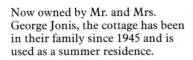

Now owned by Mr. and Mrs. George Jonis, the cottage has been in their family since 1945 and is used as a summer residence.

Compare the current image with this 1890s view; other than a color change, the cottage retains its original characteristics. The bearded man in front may be Captain Philips with his children.

The engraved front door still retains the name of the first owner.

This interior view of the parlor demonstrates the craftsmanship that went into hand painting the ceiling and walls.

15 John Wesley Way.

This cottage at 16 John Wesley Way is similar to numbers 10 and 12.

17 John Wesley Way.

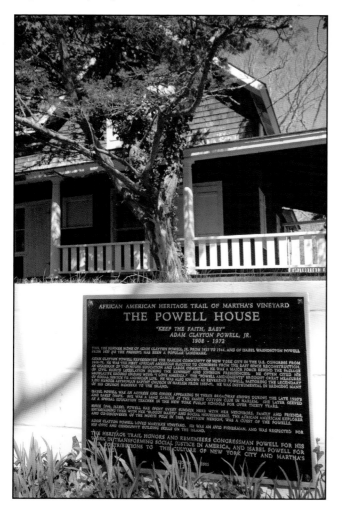

"The Bunny House" on Dorothy West Way was owned by Adam Clayton Powell, who is commemorated with this plaque. The first African American to be elected to Congress since Reconstruction, Powell was instrumental in the passage of civil rights legislation during the 1960s and 70s. "Keep The Faith Baby," is written on the sign just above Powell's name.

Admiral Benbow Inn

The Admiral Benbow Inn, located at 51 New York Avenue in the Highlands, was originally built in 1892 by A.G. Wesley, the builder and owner of the Wesley Hotel.

With its Queen Anne style of architecture, the house features a hipped roof with a windowed observatory, intersecting gables, stained glass windows, and decorative cut shingles. The first floor porch has highly stylized turned posts.

Sitting on the highest point of land overlooking Oak

Bluffs, the house was part of Vineyard Grove, where the Baptists held their camp meetings. Now owned by Bill and Mary Moore and open year round, the Admiral Benbow has seven comfortable rooms in Victorian splendor available to guests.

Porch detail.

Stained glass windows can be found throughout the house.

One of the Victorian style bedrooms.

137

Oak Bluffs

The Martha's Vineyard Land and Wharf Company

With the popularity of the famed Methodist meeting camp, six men formed a partnership in 1866 called The Martha's Vineyard Land and Wharf Company, hoping to profit by building a secular resort near the Campground. Their first purchase was a seventy-five acre parcel that bordered the Campground and extended east to Vineyard Sound. With the aid of landscape designer Robert M. Copeland, the Land and Wharf Company planned to divide the area into one thousand house lots, significantly larger than those found in the Campground. Of historic interest, this plan may very well have been the first designed residential community in the United States.

Ocean Park with its gazebo consists of seven acres facing the Sound and is surrounded by the largest and fanciest cottages. Using a central focal point and radiating roads, Copeland tried to emulate the Campground's design. In 1867, the Land and Wharf Company built a wharf extending into Nantucket Sound that would provide access to as many as fifteen steamers a day. Building was slow to begin and in 1868, only twelve cottages and thirty tents were occupied, but by 1869, almost sixty cottages had been erected.

The Arcade, designed by S.F. Pratt, was constructed in 1871 on Circuit Avenue, and housed the offices of the company as well as the post office. The Union Chapel, also designed by Pratt, was built and dedicated in August 1872 for worshippers of all faiths. It remains today a center of ecumenical activities during the summer season. Of the many hotels built to house the influx of visitors, few remain today. With the additional purchase of forty-five acres, The Land and Wharf Company owned and developed what is now Oak Bluffs.

Visitors to Martha's Vineyard are welcomed to the resort town of Oak Bluffs.

This postcard image from the early 1900s shows the New Bedford Martha's Vineyard Steamboat Co. dock, whose ships brought passengers to the island several times a day. One suggested reason why the Campground became so successful was that the only way to get there was by boat. (*Beyle Collection*)

This even earlier postcard view shows the dock and the town behind, with a large hotel beyond the bow of the steamer. The building to the left may be The United Methodist Church; the cross on the Tabernacle was not built until 1926. *(Beyle Collection)*

Early visitors to Oak Bluffs could tour and see the sites in a horse-drawn straw lined wagon, as shown in this early postcard. *(Beyle Collection)*

Newport – S. F. Pratt

Samuel Freeman (S.F.) Pratt, the architect of numerous buildings in Oak Bluffs in the 1870s, lived for almost fifty years at Bird's Nest Cottage, a house he designed at 49 Bellevue Ave, Newport, Rhode Island. Born in Cohasset, Massachusetts in 1825, the son of a carpenter, S.F. was living in Boston by 1860, his occupation listed as a carver. At some point, with several patents already to his credit, he invented a device used in sewing machines that allowed him to retire and pursue other activities, including architectural design. One of the first cottages he designed was at 1 Pequot Ave., Oak Bluffs, Martha's Vineyard, built in 1871-1872 for the governor of Massachusetts, William A. Claflin. Except for some minor details, S.F.'s own cottage in Newport, where the exterior has been restored by the present owner, was the same design as that of the governor's, which is now the Oak House B&B, located on Seaview Ave.

The Oak House has been drastically renovated with a middle floor added and most of the unique exterior designs elements no longer present. What is interesting is that the exterior of the Newport house and the interior of the Oak Bluffs house taken together provide a facsimile of the two similar cottages built in the early 1870s. While working for the Oak Bluffs Land and Wharf Company, Pratt designed more than twenty buildings in Oak Bluffs, including Union Chapel, The Arcade, Seaview Hotel, and several distinctive cottages. One of New England's major architects, Pratt died on Sept 20th, 1920, at the age of ninety-four, leaving behind a significant legacy of Victorian design.

The door at 49 Bellevue Avenue has been moved to the side of the cottage but still retains the original design.

This view of the second floor porch displays the variety of geometric shapes and angles typical of S.F. Pratt's designs. Notice that the doors from the outside appear to have a slope from the center to the outside.

Continuity of design has been maintained in this window.

The first floor porch railing design is also repeated on the second floor. Compare this pattern to other cottages found in the Campground.

From the inside, the doors are rectangular, but the glass has been cut at an angle so that it matches the outside trim.

A purple doorknob.

A triangular window faces the park.

The Arcade

The Arcade, at 32 Circuit Avenue, was the first significant building constructed by the Land and Wharf Company and was used to house their offices. Designed by S.F. Pratt, the Arcade's geometry of shapes, angles, and rooflines can be seen in Pratt's other buildings in Oak Bluffs. Circuit Avenue became the commercial center of Oak Bluffs, with the Arcade having the post office and library as occupants. In 1980, a restoration was undertaken to bring the building back to its original condition. Compare current views with the early 1900s image, and you can see how successful that restoration was.

The interior of the three-story building has changed, with the upper floors now converted to apartments and the first floor containing commercial establishments. The façade is ornate, featuring vergeboard, decorated railings, and window treatments. The other sides of the building are utilitarian with regard to doors and windows. The Arcade was added to the National Register of Historic Places in 1990.

An early postcard image showing Circuit Avenue and the Arcade on the left. (*Beyle Collection*)

The first floor opening in the Arcade leads to Montgomery Square and the Campground. The ogival double doors on the second floor porch with sidelights are covered with cut out decorated pediments.

The second and third floor porches reflect the spatial relationships that S.F. Pratt used in his designs. The oculus window on the third floor is balanced with two side windows and vergeboard that opens onto it.

This second floor window fits neatly within porch and roof lines.

Union Chapel

The Oak Bluffs Christian Union Chapel, better known as the Union Chapel, was built in 1870 and dedicated in August 1871 with eight clergymen of various denominations and a congregation that included not only locals but members of the Methodist Campground Meeting Association. As noted earlier, with the success and popularity of Wesleyan Grove, several developers had purchased an additional 75 acres of undeveloped land outside the Campground, formed the Oak Bluffs Land and Wharf Company, and with the assistance of Robert Morris Copeland (a contemporary of Fredrick Law Olmstead), designed a plan for this area that included Ocean Park, Union Chapel, and a series of radiating streets with larger lot sizes and cottages. Union Chapel was built as a non-denominational house of worship for those wandering souls not associated with the Campground.

Designed by S.F. Pratt and located at the intersection of Circuit Ave., Kennebec Ave., Narragansett Ave., and Grove St., it is the only existing octagonal building on Martha's Vineyard. Now covered with cedar shingles and having lost some of the 1870 detailing, the Chapel still retains its original picturesque form. Built in a Stick Style design, the building is 20 feet on each side and has four alternating entrances with large double doors. Stained glass triangular windows remain on the upper roof but the original ogival windows in the eight-sided clerestory have been replaced with rectangular windows. Gothic first floor windows have also been replaced.

In June 1990, Union Chapel was added to the National Register of Historic Places. A restoration project is underway to restore the sanctuary, now owned by the Martha's Vineyard Preservation Trust, to its original design and architecture. It still remains a house of worship during the summer and a location for weddings, baptisms, and special musical events.

This 1910 postcard image shows Union Chapel with its original architecture, including the bell tower and steeple with an ornate spire that reached 96 feet. After falling into disrepair, the tower was removed; the spire was a victim of the 1938 hurricane. The decorative finials on top of the diamond paned triangular windows have also been lost. In addition, the original lower level windows have been replaced with newer rectangular structures. The outside walls, originally featuring vertical boards that enhanced the geometry of the building, are now covered with shingles. Entrances have also been modified, but angles in rooflines maintain the original geometry.

A stained glass window found in the Union Chapel.

150

The ceiling of Union Chapel, built in Stick Style, is octagonal in shape with geometric windows. The four lower outer windows are in the clerestory, and the eight triangular windows extend above the roof.

The 1923 Austin organ has 1200 pipes.

With no pews, the chapel uses wicker chairs for seating and can accommodate up to 350 people. The stairs in the back lead to the eight-sided balcony; two of the four entrances can be seen.

This view of the stage and the balcony, which can seat 150, reflects the non-denominational nature of the building.

Flying Horses Carousel

A visit to the Martha's Vineyard Campground is not complete without a trip to and a ride on the Victorian Age Flying Horses carousel. Originally operated on Coney Island, the ride was brought to Cottage City in 1884 by Mr. F.O. Gordon. In 1889, the carousel was purchased by the town and moved to its present location at 15 Lake Ave. In 1896, Mr. Joseph Turnell bought the carousel and changed the name to Flying Horses, although the horses are stationary and have never moved up and down as in modern carousels. In 1979, the carousel was listed on the National Register of Historic Places and it is now owned by the Martha's Vineyard Preservation Trust, which operates the ride daily during the summer.

The carousel, which consists of twenty prancing horses and four chariots, measures 36 feet in diameter and has fourteen spreaders for support. A ten hp belt-driven motor located in the basement powers the carousel, and local scenes painted on panels decorate the central area that hides the machinery.

Original horses for the carousel, chosen from the 1878 Charles W. F. Dare catalog for amusement rides, came with real horsehair tails and mane, and large oxide eyes with small animals embedded in the center. The horses cost from $25 to $35, depending on their condition and perfection of finish. The chariots cost from $12 to $18, and could be ordered to resemble birds, dragons, or serpents.

Grab the brass ring and win a free ride.

154

This pre 1900 image shows the Flying Horse Carousel with buildings that no longer exist.

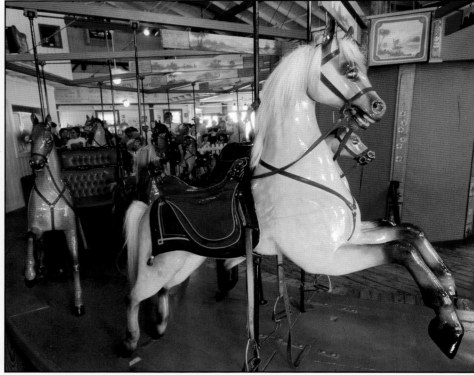

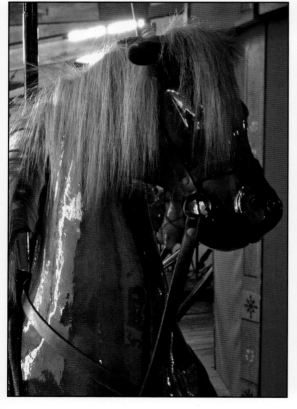

Painted panels on the carousel depict colorful local scenes.

Ocean Park

When the Land and Wharf Company designed the area outside the Campground, large lots and spacious parks on curving avenues were the objective. Ocean Park, a seven-acre grassy commons facing Nantucket Sound, was the most significant result. The original bandstand hosts summer band concerts, and the area is a hubbub of seasonal activities. Fireworks displays are held here; in 1874, President Grant watched from a nearby cottage. The cottages facing Ocean Park are the largest and most ornate in Oak Bluffs. Most have been restored to their original condition. Some still are only for summer use.

Compare the previous image with this early 1900s postcard view and notice the few changes. To the left of the bandstand is the Corbin residence (see pages 163-165).

This view of the bandstand shows one end of Ocean Avenue and the largest cottages.

In this view facing west, Nantucket Sound can be seen beyond
the bandstand with more Ocean Avenue cottages to the left.

Dr. Tucker's Cottage

Dr. Harrison Tucker's cottage at 42 Ocean Avenue was originally constructed in 1872 and significantly renovated in 1877 with its Queen Anne modifications; at that time, it was one of the most ornate and decorated cottages in Oak Bluffs. It still remains one of the most impressive cottages on Ocean Ave. Built on a parcel of four lots measuring 70 feet by 130 feet, this Stick Style residence was more pretentious than any of the other cottages of its time. With its excesses and ornate resort architecture, the cottage's carvings included sixty doves, over sixty lion heads, twelve falcons, two dragons, over one hundred and forty flowers, four John the Baptists, and twelve wolves and goats. Similar designs can be found on several other cottages throughout Oak Bluffs and in the Campground, but they do not compare with the abundance found on the Dr. Tucker cottage.

Dr. Tucker, who was born in Norton, Massachusetts, and educated at Harvard and the University of Pennsylvania medical schools, was best known for discovering, compounding, and marketing patent medicines. His most popular medicine was Diaphoretic #591, which was for the treatment of nervousness, headache, convulsions, and gum disease. With his success and the empire that followed, Dr. Tucker built opulent residences and contributed to numerous philanthropic causes, including Oak Bluffs, where he was instrumental in forming The Oak Bluffs Club and The Martha's Vineyard Club. Incorporated in 1886, the two social clubs provided entertainment and activities for prominent residents involved in civic improvement.

Dr. Tucker passed away in May of 1891 in Oak Bluffs. Dr. Tucker's Cottage was added to the National Register of Historic Places in 1990.

An 1890s stereoview image shows the Dr. Tucker cottage among the trees with several occupants on the porch. The third floor observation balcony with its numerous carvings might have been where President Grant, his wife, and the Tuckers watched fireworks in August 1874.

This porch detail shows some of the ornate carvings and the birds in the railing.

The roof, less ornate than it was in the past, still commands a magnificent view of Ocean Park and Nantucket Sound beyond.

Corbin-Norton

Built in 1891 by Philip Corbin, who owned the Corbin Lock Company, this was one of the most luxurious cottages on Ocean Avenue. Destroyed by a fire in 2001, the house has been totally restored by Peter and Eileen Norton.

The detail can be seen on the side of the house.

The geometry of roof lines and the two tone color scheme add to the elegance of the cottage.

164

Compare these two views, both showing the front of 89 Ocean Avenue but taken more than one hundred years apart. How many differences can you find?

The three story tower.

This early postcard image of Ocean Avenue looking south shows the ornate cottages facing Ocean Park. Forming a semi-circle around the seven-acre Ocean Park, Ocean Avenue cottages were built starting in 1868 in the Queen Anne and Gothic Revival styles. The largest and most prestigious cottages with extensive trim and decorations faced Nantucket Sound across the park. Notice the trolley tracks (which can also be seen in a Wesley Hotel view) that provided transportation for residents and visitors. (*Beyle Collection*)

Another early postcard image, looking north on Ocean Avenue. The first cottage is easily recognizable as number 79 and the tower towards the right is number 73, which is still present today. Directly behind this view is the Corbin-Norton cottage, and to the right would be the bandstand in the park. (*Beyle Collection*)

Comparing this view with the earlier version, one can see that many of the cottages are still recognizable with their rooflines, porches, and towers. The orange roof on the last cottage is the Dr. Tucker cottage.

Compare this image to the first view of Ocean Avenue and note the changes that have occurred.

This row of cottages faces Ocean Park.

19 Ocean Avenue is a two story cottage that has moved the front door to the side.

Porch detail for 19 Ocean Avenue.

23 Ocean avenue is a brightly colored cottage with a four-sided roof covering the second floor porch.

The porch design in the center is copied as cut-outs throughout the trim; the overlapping shingle pattern is also unique.

More details can be seen in this view of the porch and railing.

25 Ocean Avenue has the same roof line as number 23, but it wasn't extended to cover the porch.

The upper trim on the porch resembles spokes of a wheel.

35 Ocean Avenue has a three-sided porch roof with a geometric trim pattern.

The trim around the windows and doors is similar to that found in the Campground.

37 Ocean Avenue has two second floor porches—a five-sided porch on the front and a three-sided porch on the side.

The porch railing has cutout horses such as those found on the carousel.

"Sol E Mar" at 47 Ocean Avenue, with its expansive porch, dormered windows, and unique tower, catches the sun and faces the sea.

The cottage at 49 Ocean Avenue was built in 1890 in the Campground and then moved to this location, which was originally a tent site. Owned by Mr. and Mrs. Raymond Santinello, the cottage has not been winterized and is only used during the summer season.

57 Ocean Avenue, with its distinctive peaked roof, also has turned posts on the first floor.

With three stripes in the roof, 51 Ocean Avenue features rounded windows and doors, overlapping shingles, and animals in the vergeboard.

71 Ocean Avenue.

Though modernized and with a color change, this cottage at number 73 with a four story tower can still be recognized from the earlier image of Ocean Avenue.

Bright yellow with two shades of green, 79 Ocean Avenue is a large two story cottage.

The variations in rooflines can be seen in this side view.

This large restored cottage at 89 Ocean Avenue looks the same as it did one hundred years ago. Compare it to the old view of the bandstand in Ocean Park.

91 Ocean Avenue has also been totally restored, and other than a color change looks the same as it did over one hundred years ago.

Oak House

The Oak House on Seaview Avenue facing Vineyard Sound is a ten room bed and breakfast that has been significantly renovated from its original condition. Designed by S.F. Pratt, this cottage was built the same year (1872) as Pratt's Bird's Nest Cottage in Newport, and a comparison of the two shows similarities in architecture. In the mid 1870s, the cottage was the summer residence of Massachusetts Governor William Claflin, who made significant changes to both the interior with marble sinks and oak paneling, and to the exterior with balconies and porches.

The bedrooms with the oak paneling are reminiscent of a hundred and thirty years ago.

Samoset Avenue

Samoset Avenue is the next street behind Ocean Avenue and has large decorated cottages. This view is towards Seaview Avenue and Nantucket Sound beyond.

6 Samoset Avenue.

An arched porch entrance and a six-sided tower at 10 Samoset Avenue.

181

16 Samoset Avenue was designed by S.F. Pratt and has several distinctive characteristics, including the tower and whale rib rings.

Compare this front view and the whale ribs on the house.

Close up porch detail.

The second floor porch and tower.

Built in 1875, 18 Samoset Avenue has been owned by the same family for over eighty years.

This interior view of the living room is facing the street.

The distinctive partition trim can be seen between the living room and back room.

Cinderella Cottage

Built in 1881, the Cinderella Cottage at 36 Peqout Avenue, originally known as the Legg cottage, has been meticulously restored to its previous condition.

Porch trim and detail on the first floor.

Distinctive trim on the second floor porch.

33 Pequot Avenue was probably designed by S.F. Pratt, who also designed the Arcade and Union Chapel.

In this porch view, the Cinderella Cottage can partially be seen in the background.

The etched glass in the rounded windows is a characteristic found in many cottages.

35 Pequot Avenue has a wrap around first floor porch.

This porch detail shows Hartford Park and open space between the houses across the street.

37 Pequot Avenue has complementary flowers to match
the cottage color and a screened in second floor porch.

Far left:
Porch detail of the Crystal Palace.

Left:
Distinctive and noteworthy in this view of the tower are the shingles, windows, and trim.

45 Pequot Avenue was built in 1869 by Henry C. Clark, a Providence coal merchant, and is known as The Crystal Palace. In 1875, this cottage was moved from its original location in Trinity Park opposite the Campground Museum to its present location in Hartford Park.

Cottagers' Corner

This early 1900s postcard shows the park and Cottagers' Corner to the left.

Built in 1892 as the Cottage City Town Hall and located on the corner of Pequot Avenue and Grove Avenue, this building is now the home of the Cottagers Inc., a philanthropic group of women who support island charities.

Narragansett Avenue

An early postcard image of Narragansett Avenue with Nantucket Sound in the background. This street has numerous expansive cottages. *(Beyle Collection)*

As seen in this early postcard, Narragansett Avenue in this direction joins Circuit Avenue at the Union Chapel. *(Beyle Collection)*

7 Narragansett Avenue.

Quite ornate with a tower and numerous decorative trim, 19 Narragansett Avenue has been beautifully restored.

32 Narragansett Avenue.

This cottage is at 28 Narragansett Avenue.

The second floor porch is supported by a three-sided extension with rounded and etched windows.

39 Narragansett Avenue.

41 Narragansett
Avenue.

48 Narragansett Avenue.

The front doors of 50 Narragansett Avenue.

The Narragansett House at 46 Narragansett Avenue was one of the first buildings designed and built as a hotel in Oak Bluffs, and has been in continuous operation since the late 1860s. Brightly colored in a distinctive pink and blue, the bed and breakfast, now owned and operated by Jane and Paul Lofgren, has thirteen rooms available for seasonal visitors.

The windows and doors have the distinctive shape and trim of the original construction.

This bedroom found in one of the peaks has a rounded window.

Another bedroom leads to a porch.

Painted bright green, this cottage at 27 Naumkeeg Avenue has closed in vergeboard on the gable of the roof.

Porch detail.

Porch detail shows the highly stylized vergeboard.

This large cottage at 32 Penacook Avenue has a wraparound first floor porch and dormered second floor windows.

48 Penacook Avenue has been expanded with an addition in the rear.

White with blue trim and scalloped shingles, this cottage is at 56 Penacook Avenue.

Featuring two oculus windows on the second floor porch, this pink cottage
at 28 Massasoit Avenue has a portico entrance and partially enclosed porch.

A Winter Medley

In winter, with a covering of snow, the Campground is peaceful and quiet. Since only about 50 of the 300 cottages have been winterized, it is possible to witness the beauty and character of the area. The Association maintains the roads and pathways and keeps them free of snow. With no leaves on the trees, the close proximity of the Tabernacle and the cottages is more evident, and one can see how pervasive the community spirit is during the summer season. The following images were taken in various areas throughout the Campground and can be compared to other images found in this book taken during the summer.

The Trinity Methodist Church is open for services year round.

The Tabernacle and Trinity Church within the central area of Trinity Park.

4 and 5 Trinity Park.

6, 8 and 10 Trinity Park.

A Campground cottage.

Trinity Park cottages 22 to25.

30 Trinity Park was built in 1875.

22 Trinity Park.

12 Vincent Park.

These cottages are in Wesleyan Grove.

20 Trinity Park porch.

Vincent Park.

This cottage in Trinity Park
was built in 1867.

1 Bayliss Avenue.

Bibliography

Note: This book is a photographic presentation of Victorian Age homes and buildings in Oak Bluffs, Massachusetts, as they presently exist. More than merely a group of cottages, the Campground has had a treasured history for over 160 years. Besides the materials listed below, numerous resources are available to those who wish to pursue further study of this area. The Martha's Vineyard Campmeeting Association (www.mvcma.org) and The Martha's Vineyard Historical Society (www.marthasvineyardhistory.org) are both invaluable organizations for seeking additional information.

Corsiglia, Betsy, and Mary-Jean Miner. *Unbroken Circles: The Campground of Martha's Vineyard.* Boston: David R. Godine, 2000.

"Historic Walking Tour of Oak Bluffs." (Brochure, originally produced by the Oak Bluffs Centennial Committee and the Oak Bluffs Historical Commission, 1980. Text expanded from original by Jill Bouck and Sara Nevin.)

Hough, Henry Beetle. "Camp Meeting of 1872." *The Dukes County Intelligencer* 29, November 1987, 64-71.

Martha's Vineyard Camp Meeting Association. "A Brief History and Map of the Martha's Vineyard Camp-Meeting Association." (Brochure, c. 2005)

"Martha's Vineyard Camp Meeting Association 1835." (Brochure, with information obtained from *Martha's Vineyard Camp Meeting Association 1835-1985*, compiled and written by Sally W. Dagnall)

"Map of Oak Bluffs: Complete Guide." Published by Oak Bluffs Association, Oak Bluffs, MA, c. 2005.

Senter, Oramel. "Oak Bluffs: An 1877 Travel Guide." *The Dukes County Intelligencer* 21 May 1980. 133-143.

Weiss, Ellen. "The Iron Tabernacle at Wesleyan Grove." *The Dukes County Intelligencer* 21. August 1979, 3-14.

Weiss, Ellen. "Samuel Freeman Pratt: An Architect of Oak Bluffs." *The Dukes County Intelligencer* 21. May 1980. 123 -132

Weiss, Ellen. *City in the Woods, The Life and Design of an American Camp Meeting on Martha's Vineyard. Second Edition.* Boston: Northeastern University Press, 1998.

Index